NATIONAL GEOGRAPHIC

Ladders

TRICKS, TRAPS, AND TOOLS

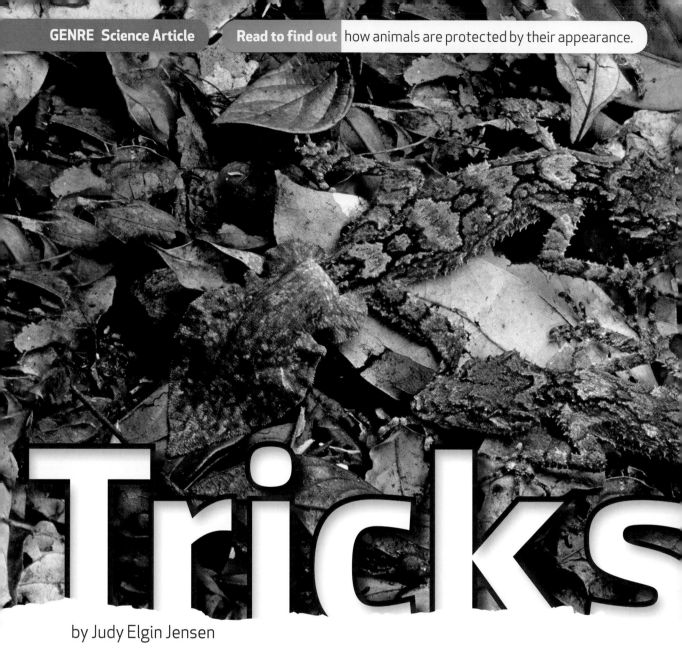

Tricks

by Judy Elgin Jensen

Imagine a rain forest in Queensland, Australia. Dead brown leaves cover the ground. But look closely. Are they all *really* leaves? Some things in nature may look like something else.

Several leaf-tailed geckos hide in the leaves. They are colored and shaped like leaves. Even their tails look like leaves. The geckos keep still as they watch for insects to eat. **Predators** that want to eat the geckos cannot see them easily.

How many leaf-tailed geckos can you find? The background has been lightened to make it easier to see one of them.

On the ground, these geckos are the same color. Soon they will climb up different trees. There each gecko's coloring will change. Then they will all look different.

Have you found the leaf-tailed geckos yet? Look closely. There are three of them.

Hiding in Plain Sight

Many animals use **camouflage** for protection. Their skins, shells, fur, or feathers look like their surroundings. It is hard for a predator to see these animals. Some predators use camouflage to hide from prey. Then they can catch and eat the prey.

Jagged Ambush Bug
Where it lives: Eastern North America
What's special: This bug sits on flowers. It waits for an insect to land. Then the bug grabs the insect and kills it with poison. The bug often attacks larger insects. Do you see the bug? It is green and brown.

Malaysian Orchid Mantis
Where it lives: Rain forests in Malaysia
What's special: This mantis looks like a flower called an orchid. Some mantises are pink or purple just like some orchids. Can you find the mantis's dark eyes?

Soft Coral Crab
Where it lives: Coral reefs near Indonesia
What's special: This crab lives among coral polyps. Look for the crab's spiny legs with pink stripes.

Looking Dangerous

Camouflage is only one way animals survive. Many dangerous animals have bright colors or patterns. Predators avoid these animals. Some harmless animals mimic, or copy, dangerous animals. They have the same bright colors and patterns. This **mimicry** keeps them safe.

Model: Plain Tiger Butterfly

The plain tiger caterpillar eats leaves. The leaves make the adult taste bad. The adult also smells bad to predators.

Mimic: Danaid Eggfly Butterfly

The female danaid eggfly looks like a plain tiger. But this butterfly does not taste bad. Even so, predators stay away from it.

Model: Yellowjacket

The yellowjacket wasp can give predators a painful sting.

Mimic: Yellowjacket Hover Fly

This hover fly doesn't sting. But it looks like a yellowjacket. It sounds like one, too.

Model: Coral Snake

The coral snake is poisonous. It has yellow, black, and red bands. Its bands say, "Watch out!" The scarlet king snake is not poisonous. But it has yellow, black, and red bands, too. Predators know coral snakes can make them sick. So they also stay away from the banded scarlet king snake.

Mimic: Scarlet King Snake

Confusing Predators

Some animals confuse predators. They may puff up their bodies to look bigger. Some have markings that make them look like larger animals.

Io Moth

The io moth (above) spreads its wings. It has big black eyespots. To predators, its spots look like the eyes of an owl (to the right).

Puss Moth Caterpillar
The caterpillar of the European puss moth confuses predators. When it is startled, it pulls its head into its body. It rears up. The front of its body looks like a big red "mouth." The caterpillar's tails can also squirt acid at predators!

Some animals use camouflage to hide from predators. Other animals have colors and patterns that keep predators away. The goal is always survival.

Check In How does mimicry protect an animal from predators?

Trap

by Judy Elgin Jensen

A frog hops among the sticky sundew plants. Oops! Too close. Now the frog is stuck to a plant. The sticky liquid will smother the frog. Then the frog will become soup for the plant.

Plants make their food using sunlight. Plants also need **nutrients** from the soil. In many swamps and bogs, the soil does not contain enough nutrients. There, **carnivorous plants** get nutrients by trapping small animals.

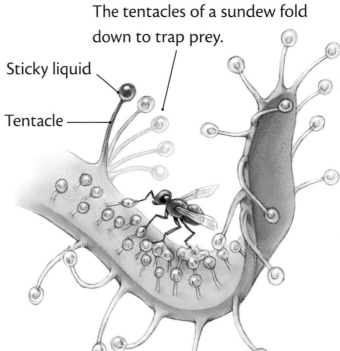

The tentacles of a sundew fold down to trap prey.

Sticky liquid

Tentacle

This frog is caught in a sticky sundew plant.

Sundews

There are many kinds of sundew plants. Some are tiny. Others are taller than you! Sundew leaves may grow in a circle or on stalks. Thick hairs, or tentacles, cover the leaves. Sticky liquid on each tentacle traps and digests animals.

Bladderworts

A plant with tiny "bubbles" floats in a pond. A small animal swims by. It touches trigger hairs on a bubble. WHOOSH! The water around the animal is sucked inside the bubble. The animal is sucked in, too. That bubble was a trap!

The trap slams shut. Digestive juices fill the trap. Goodbye tiny animal.

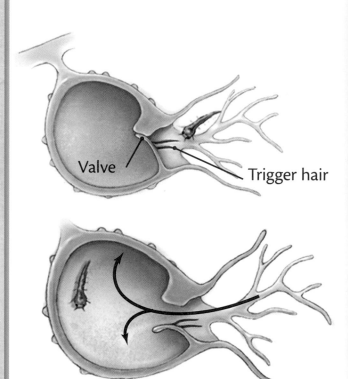

Valve

Trigger hair

^ The bladderwort pumps water out of its trap. If an animal touches a trigger hair, the trap opens. Water rushes in. The animal goes in, too.

< Bladderworts don't have roots to get nutrients from soil. Instead they get their nutrients from tiny animals.

Venus Flytraps

Venus flytraps catch small animals that crawl across their leaves. Each leaf has trigger hairs. If an animal touches the trigger hairs, the leaf snaps shut. It traps the animal and digests it. Then the leaf opens again, ready for its next meal.

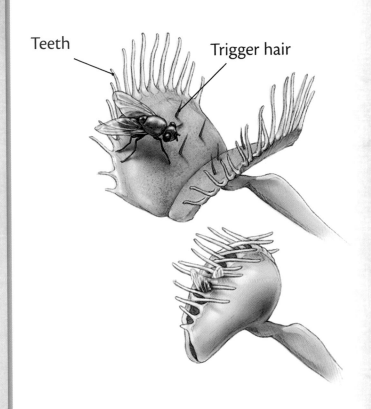

Teeth

Trigger hair

When an insect walks across a Venus flytrap leaf, it touches the trigger hairs. That causes the two halves of the leaf to snap shut.

Pitcher Plants

A pitcher-shaped leaf smells like nectar. An ant leans in for a sip. It slips and slides down the inside of the pitcher. At the bottom is a pool of water and digestive fluid. The ant drowns. Its body breaks down. The plant gets nutrients from the ant's body.

As the ant tries to crawl out of the pitcher, it runs into hairs that point downward. The hairs act as spears and keep the ant in the pool.

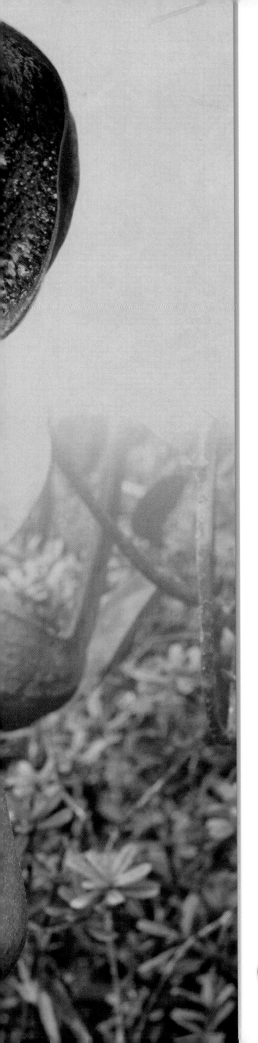

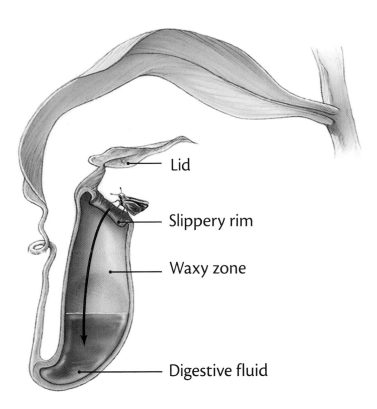

Lid

Slippery rim

Waxy zone

Digestive fluid

In some places, the soil does not have enough nutrients. Most plants cannot grow there. But carnivorous plants thrive. Their bodies trap and digest small animals. This gives carnivorous plants the nutrients they need.

Yum. Bug juice.

Check In   How does the leaf of a pitcher plant trap an ant?

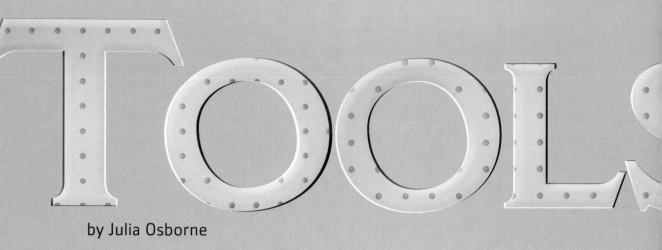

TOOLS

by Julia Osborne

Humans use many different tools. The tools may be simple, such as spoons. They may be complex, such as computers. Tools are objects used to carry out a task.

Scientists once thought only humans were able to use tools. But that idea is changing.

An Egyptian vulture picks up a small egg and drops it. The egg breaks. The vulture slurps up the insides. An ostrich egg is too big to pick up and drop. Instead, the vulture throws stones at the egg. The stones break the egg. The vulture is using the stones as tools.

Read on to learn how some animals use objects to do jobs or change their environment.

An Eyptian vulture drops a stone on an egg.

The sound of rushing water triggers a special behavior in a beaver. It builds a dam. The dam holds back the water, making a pond.

Using Instinct

All animals perform complex actions called **behaviors.** Some animals act by **instinct,** without learning or being taught. Animals inherit instincts from their parents.

Instinct guides the behavior of beavers. Beavers cut down trees. They use the sticks and mud to build lodges in ponds. The lodges keep the beavers safe from predators.

What if there is no pond? Beavers use sticks and mud to build a dam across a stream. The dam blocks the moving water. Now the beavers have a pond. Sticks and mud are tools. They change the beavers' environment.

Do young beavers learn from adults? Scientists watched young beavers that had been raised without adults. These beavers built a dam. It looked just like the dams built by adult beavers. Scientists had the answer to their question. Building dams is an instinct.

> This capuchin monkey is cracking a nut.

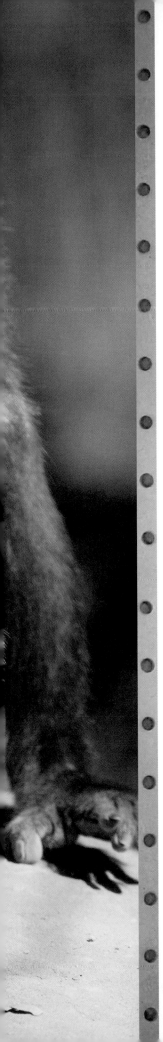

Learning to Use Tools

You once learned to use a spoon to eat. Many young animals also learn to use tools. Wild capuchin [KAP-yu-chin] monkeys learn to crack nuts with stones. Then they eat the meat inside. Cracking nuts is a learned behavior.

Very young capuchins watch the nut-cracking behavior of other monkeys. They practice for a few years before they become experts. Baby monkeys beat stones against things. One-year-olds start trying to crack nuts. By about age three, young monkeys are able to crack nuts with a stone.

Sometimes adult monkeys join the group. These adults do not know how to crack nuts. They learn the skill by watching other monkeys and practicing on their own.

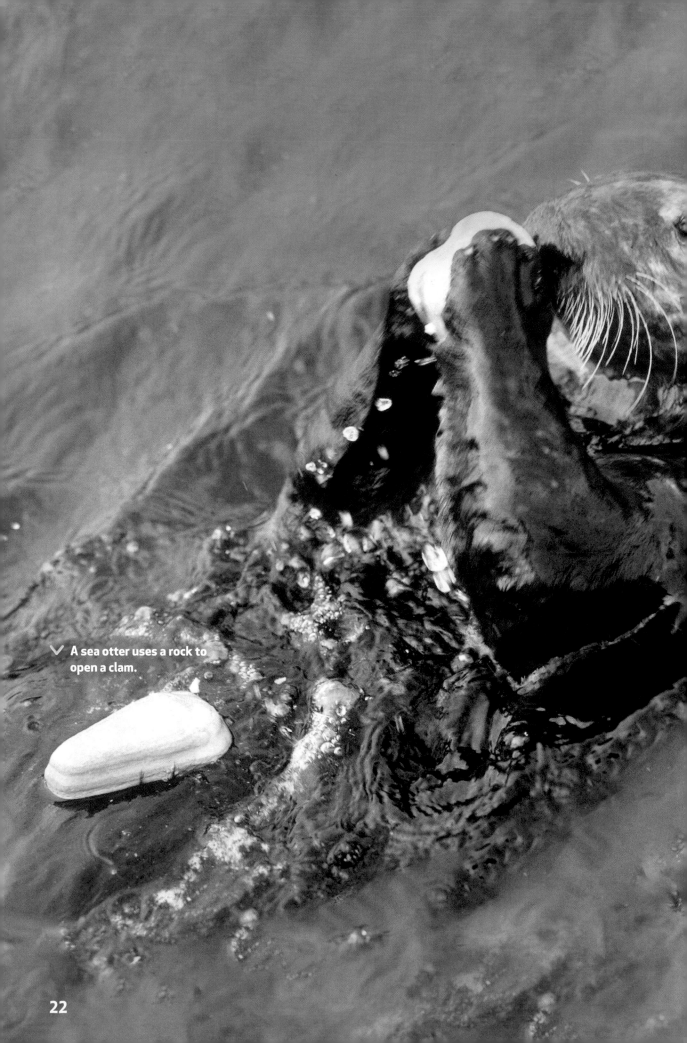

∨ A sea otter uses a rock to open a clam.

Water Crackers

Furry sea otters hunt, eat, and sleep in the ocean. Often, they float on their backs.

Some sea otters have learned to use rocks as tools. When the otter gets hungry, it dives to the ocean floor. There it picks up a clam. It also picks up a rock.

The otter floats on its back with the rock on its belly. Then it smashes the clam against the rock. The clamshell cracks open. U-m-m-m-m. A tasty snack.

Scientists have learned a lot about how animals use tools. Some animals know how to use tools by instinct. Others learn to use tools by watching or by trying on their own.

Check In   What is the difference between an instinct and a learned behavior?

Discuss

1. The three pieces in this book are "Tricks," "Traps," and "Tools." Describe some of the ways these three pieces are connected.

2. Think about the animals in "Tricks." What are some ways that their shapes and colors protect them from predators?

3. Compare the actions of the sundew plant in "Traps" with the behavior of the ambush bug in "Tricks." How are they alike and different?

4. Describe how capuchin monkeys learn to open nuts.

5. What else would you like to know about the plants and animals in this book? How could you find out more?